AI POWERED IMPACT

Transformative Applications in Supply Chain Healthcare & Supply Chain

Aishat Olatunji

Dedication

To every thinker, builder, and problem solver who chooses to lead with clarity in a world driven by complexity.

To the quiet innovators working behind the scenes, whose contributions never make headlines but transform systems every day.

And most personally, to my family whose support has been unwavering, whose belief has been unshakable, and whose love has been my foundation.

This work reflects the lessons I have learned, the questions I continue to ask, and the journey we are all on toward meaningful, intelligent impact.

Table Of Contents

Foreword

The era of artificial intelligence is not on the horizon. It is already here. Across industries and sectors, we are witnessing a significant shift in how decisions are made, operations are managed, and value is created. Yet among the excitement, what remains absent in many conversations is clarity. Not just about what artificial intelligence is, but how it can be used with purpose, structure, and integrity to build systems that perform better for businesses, for individuals, and for society.

This book, *AI Powered Impact*, arrives at a defining moment. It is not just a response to technological change but a clear framework for using that change intelligently. What makes this work exceptional is not only its technical depth but also its practical relevance. Aishat Olatunji combines engineering precision with real world insight, showing how artificial intelligence can be applied to solve pressing problems in supply chain, healthcare, and supply chain.

With experience rooted in execution, she explains how tools such as machine learning, predictive analytics, and natural language processing can be designed to unlock efficiency, reduce risk, and empower leadership. This book does not chase trends. It sets a new standard for how innovation should be built and applied in complex systems.

By reading this, you are not simply consuming information. You are entering a space where intelligent systems are guided by ethical thinking, strong vision, and technical excellence. Whether you are a data scientist, a business executive, a student, or a policymaker, this book gives you the confidence to navigate and lead in a world shaped by artificial intelligence.

I strongly recommend this work to anyone who seeks to understand and shape the future with intention and clarity. It is relevant, necessary, and most importantly, ready to be applied.

Preface

This book began as a question; how can intelligent systems truly create meaningful impact across the most complex industries? That question did not emerge in theory, but in practice. In supply chain breakdowns where time was critical, in healthcare settings where accuracy determined outcomes, and in financial environments where data moved faster than judgment. Again, I saw a need not just for more tools, but for smarter application of the tools we already had.

Over the years, I have had the opportunity to work closely with teams solving real problems using artificial intelligence, analytics, and data science. These experiences informed every chapter of this book. What you will find here is not speculation or abstract theory. It is a detailed exploration of how artificial intelligence can be designed, implemented, and scaled for measurable value. The examples are drawn from projects where results mattered, where the difference between success and failure could be seen in logistics timelines, diagnostic outcomes, or fraud detection rates.

My aim with this book is to make these insights accessible, especially to those working in environments where stakes are high and resources are limited. From graduate students and researchers to industry professionals and technology leaders, the audience I imagined while writing is as diverse as the challenges we face in this field. Artificial intelligence is a tool, but its impact is shaped by our choices, what we solve, how we build, and why we deploy.

Each chapter is structured to follow a real-world logic. First, it sets the context. Then it describes the problem. Finally, it shows how artificial intelligence and data science were used to drive improvement. The goal is not only to teach, but to equip, to make this book something that lives on desks, not just shelves.

I am grateful to every mentor, colleague, and collaborator who contributed to the thinking that shapes these pages. Your insight and challenge sharpened the work. This book is for you, and for everyone seeking clarity during complexity.

Let us now begin.

Introduction

Artificial Intelligence is no longer a theoretical abstraction or the privilege of experimental labs. It is now at the centre of how the world functions, from how we receive healthcare to how we manage global supply networks and financial risk. The demand for intelligence that is not only powerful but also practical has pushed both technology and society into an era of extraordinary possibility and responsibility.

This book was written to demystify the real-world potential of artificial intelligence and machine learning in the domains where clarity, precision, and reliability are critical. The chapters that follow draw on field-tested approaches, applied research, and project execution insights to help professionals understand not just the why, but the how of transformative AI. Whether it is predictive analytics improving logistics, natural language processing enhancing medical documentation, or machine learning models detecting fraud in financial transactions, the applications discussed here reflect the power of insight made real.

At the heart of this work is a commitment to responsible innovation. Artificial Intelligence is not magic. It is structured reasoning powered by data, sharpened by context, and shaped by human judgment. This book will walk you through systems that not only work but deliver measurable impact. It is intended for practitioners, decision makers, and those preparing to lead the next wave of digital transformation.

Welcome to a journey through intelligence that works.

Chapter 1

Foundations of AI for High Impact Industries

Artificial Intelligence has evolved from a conceptual pursuit into a practical engine of transformation across industries. At its core, AI enables machines to mimic human intelligence through learning, reasoning, and self-correction. For industries like supply chain and healthcare where complexity, data volume, and decision velocity converge AI offers a paradigm shift. It no longer serves merely as a back-end tool; it is fast becoming a central force in strategic planning, service delivery, and operational efficiency.

The foundational layer of AI lies in data. Every AI system is as effective as the data it learns from. In high-impact industries, this data is vast, often unstructured, and constantly changing.

Leveraging it requires more than storage, it requires intelligent frameworks that process, analyse, and extract meaning in real time. Techniques such as supervised learning, unsupervised clustering, and reinforcement learning allow organizations to transition from reactive problem-solving to predictive and prescriptive planning.

Another cornerstone of AI in these sectors is its ability to model uncertainty. In supply chain, for example, AI models can account for fluctuating demand, disrupted logistics, or supplier risks by using probabilistic reasoning. In healthcare, AI augments diagnostics by detecting early patterns that evade traditional clinical methods. Finance benefits from AI's pattern recognition, detecting anomalies in real-time to curb fraud. These capabilities are not theoretical—they are already shaping workflows, reengineering processes, and redefining the scope of what is possible across mission-critical sectors.

Understanding AI, Machine Learning, and Deep Learning

Artificial Intelligence has evolved from a conceptual framework into a powerful driver of innovation across industries. It refers broadly to the simulation of human intelligence by machines, enabling them to perform tasks such as reasoning, learning, perception, and problem-solving. While AI is often used as a blanket term, it comprises multiple layers of technology, each offering increasing levels of sophistication in mimicking human intelligence.

At the heart of modern AI systems lies Machine Learning, a subset of AI that empowers computers to learn from data without being explicitly programmed. Rather than relying on rigid rule-based systems, machine learning algorithms identify patterns within large datasets and use those patterns to make predictions or decisions. These algorithms improve as they are exposed to more data, offering a scalable approach to automating processes and generating insights across sectors such as supply chain management, diagnostics, and financial analysis.

Deep Learning builds upon the principles of machine learning but involves more complex structures known as neural networks. These architectures are designed to emulate the human brain's interconnected neurons and are especially effective at processing unstructured data such as images, audio, and text. In industries like healthcare, deep learning models are revolutionizing diagnostics by enabling early detection of diseases from medical scans. In finance, they are improving fraud detection by recognizing hidden anomalies in transaction data. In the supply chain, they enhance demand forecasting by analysing time-series data and environmental conditions. Together, these three fields provide the technical foundation upon which transformative applications are being built.

Core Algorithms Powering Industry Solutions

At the heart of AI-driven transformation in supply chain, healthcare, and finance lie a range of core algorithms designed to process data, identify patterns, and generate predictions or decisions. These algorithms form the engine behind intelligent systems that deliver efficiency, precision, and speed at scale. Understanding these foundational models is essential for building reliable, industry-specific AI applications.

In supply chain management, algorithms such as decision trees, support vector machines, and reinforcement learning models are used to forecast demand, optimize routing, and manage inventory dynamically. For instance, reinforcement learning enables autonomous systems to learn optimal logistics strategies through trial and error, continuously improving performance based on environmental feedback. Clustering techniques like k-means are also frequently used to segment customers, suppliers, or distribution zones to tailor operational responses more effectively.

Healthcare applications rely heavily on classification and regression algorithms. Logistic regression helps predict the likelihood of a patient developing a disease, while convolutional neural networks (CNNs) are vital for analyzing complex medical images like MRIs or CT scans. In finance, algorithms such as random forests and gradient boosting machines detect fraud, assess creditworthiness, and support algorithmic trading. Natural language processing techniques, including recurrent neural networks (RNNs) and transformer models, are also pivotal across all three sectors, enabling systems to interpret unstructured data like clinical notes, insurance records, or transaction histories. Each algorithm, carefully selected and trained, serves a distinct role in solving complex industry problems with accuracy and adaptability.

Ethical AI and Responsible Innovation

The integration of artificial intelligence into high-impact sectors like supply chain, healthcare, and finance must go beyond technical efficiency and predictive power. It demands a strong ethical framework that ensures transparency, accountability, and fairness. As AI systems increasingly influence decisions that affect human well-being and financial stability, ethical considerations are no longer optional — they are imperative.

In healthcare, ethical AI must prioritize patient privacy, informed consent, and unbiased diagnostics. Algorithms used in clinical decision-making should be interpretable and rigorously tested to avoid disparities in treatment outcomes. In supply chain management, responsible innovation involves ensuring that predictive models do not reinforce systemic inefficiencies or exploit vulnerable labour markets. Bias in sourcing data, for example, can result in skewed inventory recommendations or misaligned distribution policies that affect entire communities.

In finance, the risks of algorithmic discrimination and opaque decision systems are particularly high. Ethical AI in this space must uphold fairness in credit scoring, transparency in fraud detection, and accuracy in customer profiling. To enable responsible innovation, organizations must establish governance structures that monitor AI performance, audit training data, and evaluate societal impact regularly. Embedding ethical principles into the development lifecycle fosters trust, encourages accountability, and ensures that technological advancement contributes meaningfully to inclusive and sustainable progress across sectors.

Chapter 2

Building Scalable Data Architectures

As data becomes the foundation of modern enterprise, the need for scalable architectures has never been more pressing. Organizations across healthcare, finance, and supply chain face growing demands to collect, process, and apply insights from massive volumes of structured and unstructured data. Building scalable data architectures is therefore not only a technical challenge but a strategic requirement for competitiveness, agility, and sustained impact.

A scalable data architecture refers to the design and structure of data systems that can grow with increasing demand without performance degradation. Unlike static or siloed systems, scalable architectures are adaptive, efficient, and capable of supporting real-time decision environments. In supply chain logistics, this allows seamless coordination across warehouses, transport nodes, and vendor systems. In healthcare, it enables continuous data capture from diagnostic tools, patient records, and monitoring systems. In finance, it powers fraud detection engines, transaction analysis, and customer behaviour models.

The most effective architectures are built with clear intent. They prioritize modularity, allowing parts of the system to be updated, expanded, or reconfigured without requiring a complete overhaul. They also embrace distributed processing, ensuring data workloads are balanced across servers or nodes to prevent bottlenecks. Cloud environments play a significant role here, offering elasticity and access to computational power that is both dynamic and cost efficient. Meanwhile, organizations that require tighter control may adopt hybrid models, combining on-site servers with remote data services to balance compliance with innovation.

One critical pillar of scalable architecture is data integrity. Systems must ensure that data remains consistent, secure, and reliable across the entire pipeline. This requires robust governance frameworks, encryption protocols, and monitoring tools that flag anomalies early. In sectors like healthcare, this protects patient confidentiality while supporting advanced analytics. In supply chains, it prevents misallocation of goods or duplication of shipments. In finance, it preserves trust in digital transactions and risk modelling systems.

Another defining factor is system interoperability. Scalable architectures must be designed to integrate seamlessly with other platforms, whether internal business systems, partner technologies, or external data providers. This is especially vital in high-impact industries where collaboration between units, departments, or even nations is necessary for holistic service delivery. Designing with open standards, adaptable APIs, and flexible data models ensures the architecture supports both current operations and future needs.

Finally, building scalable data architectures demands not just technical skill but visionary leadership. The best solutions align with business strategy, anticipate future data demands, and provide room for growth. They empower teams to extract insight faster, make informed decisions, and innovate responsibly. As the digital landscape evolves, organizations that master the principles of scalable architecture will not only manage change they will lead it.

Infrastructure for AI Driven Operations

The transition from conventional data systems to intelligent, AI driven operations begin with infrastructure. Without a resilient foundation, even the most advanced algorithms fail to deliver meaningful results. Infrastructure for AI driven operations goes beyond hardware or cloud deployment; it encompasses the total environment in which machine learning models are trained, deployed, and refined. This environment must be stable, scalable, and secure, with the flexibility to support diverse workloads and constantly evolving data types.

AI driven operations depend on massive volumes of high-quality data, fast processing capabilities, and low latency in decision cycles. To meet these needs, organizations often adopt distributed computing frameworks, containerization for model portability, and orchestration tools that allow dynamic scaling of services. In practical terms, this could mean leveraging a network of processing nodes that handle data across geographic regions or utilizing container clusters that allow AI models to be updated and redeployed without disrupting services. These approaches enable enterprises to stay agile while managing cost, compliance, and system performance.

For healthcare, finance, and supply chain organizations, the infrastructure must also support real time inference. That is, it should enable AI models to make instant predictions based on new data inputs. In supply chain settings, this means adjusting inventory or routes based on traffic or demand. In healthcare, it can involve alerting physicians to early signs of patient distress. In finance, it enables flagging of suspicious transactions the moment they occur. Achieving this requires integration between data storage, compute engines, and analytics platforms, as well as strong communication protocols between system layers.

Equally important is the infrastructure's ability to support continuous learning. AI is not static; it requires constant refinement through updated datasets and real-world feedback. An effective infrastructure must include mechanisms for model retraining, validation, and deployment at scale. This might involve pipelines that automate data ingestion, labelling, and tuning processes. In highly regulated industries like healthcare and banking, these pipelines must also adhere to strict governance and audit requirements, ensuring transparency and traceability of every model decision.

Security remains a central concern in AI infrastructure. Sensitive information, whether patient data, financial records, or proprietary supply chain strategies, must be protected at all stages of processing. This necessitates encrypted data flow, access controls, and real time monitoring of system vulnerabilities. Infrastructure design must balance openness for innovation with rigorous enforcement of security policies. Only then can AI systems be trusted to operate within mission critical environments.

Ultimately, infrastructure for AI driven operations is not just about speed or storage. It is about building systems that are robust, adaptive, and capable of supporting intelligent decision making across entire organizations. With the right infrastructure in place, businesses can unlock the full power of AI not as a onetime solution, but as an enduring strategic capability.

Data Warehousing and Pipeline Efficiency

In today's data-centric landscape, success in high-impact industries depends not only on access to data but on how well that data is managed, transformed, and delivered. Data warehousing and pipeline efficiency are critical pillars that support the performance of AI-driven systems. A well-structured data warehouse does more than just store information it enables organizations to unify datasets from disparate sources and serve them up reliably for real-time analytics, forecasting, and automated decision making.

Modern warehouses must handle streaming data, adapt to evolving data structures, and support concurrent access by analytical engines. Cloud-native platforms have redefined warehousing, offering elastic scalability, robust data governance, and seamless integration with AI tools. But without efficient pipelines feeding these systems, the warehouse itself becomes static. Efficient pipelines ensure that data is not only delivered but refined cleansed, transformed, and validated before being utilized.

A pipeline is not a passive channel. It is an orchestrated system that governs how data moves, how it changes along the way, and how resilient it is against failures. In healthcare, delays in processing clinical data can hinder diagnosis. In finance, lags in transactional data may obscure fraud. In supply chains, outdated inventory data can lead to stockouts or overstock. These sectors require pipelines that are fast, fault-tolerant, and aligned with business goals.

Robust orchestration allows pipelines to run complex workflows with precision managing retries, dependencies, and load balancing automatically. Built-in observability ensures that every transformation and anomaly is logged, empowering teams to troubleshoot quickly and comply with regulatory requirements. This is especially vital in sectors where data traceability and auditability are not optional but mandated.

Data governance must also be deeply embedded. Efficient pipelines enforce privacy policies, track usage, and apply encryption from source to destination. This ensures that sensitive data—whether patient records or financial transactions—is protected at every stage. The result is a data ecosystem that is secure, transparent, and primed for responsible AI application.

Together, the data warehouse and its pipelines form the foundation of scalable intelligence. They transform static repositories into living systems capable of powering real-time insight, predictive modelling, and adaptive strategy. Without this backbone, even the most advanced AI model's falter. With it, organizations gain the confidence to trust their data and the clarity to act on it.

Scalability in Diverse Deployment Environments

Scalability is no longer a technical luxury—it is a foundational necessity. In today's complex and fast-changing business landscape, AI systems must adapt seamlessly to various deployment environments, from on-premises data centres to hybrid cloud architectures and edge computing platforms. Each environment presents unique demands, and the ability of an AI solution to scale efficiently across them determines its long-term viability.

Diverse deployment environments often reflect differences in infrastructure maturity, regulatory constraints, and operational priorities. For example, a healthcare provider may require an on-premises deployment to maintain strict control over sensitive patient data, while a retail logistics firm may prefer a cloud-based setup for its elasticity and global accessibility. AI applications must be designed with this variability in mind, ensuring that performance and security are maintained regardless of infrastructure.

True scalability means more than just running on multiple servers—it involves modular system design, containerization, and decoupled architecture that enables independent scaling of components. This flexibility allows organizations to allocate resources precisely where they are needed, whether it is processing medical imaging models, fraud detection algorithms, or real-time supply chain predictions.

Moreover, scalable systems must also be resilient. They must automatically recover from failure, adapt to changes in workload, and support versioning and rollback for continuous improvement. In industries like finance and healthcare, where downtime can have critical implications, these capabilities are non-negotiable.

Ultimately, scalable deployment ensures that AI solutions are not constrained by environment, geography, or scale. They can serve a single facility or a global enterprise with equal precision. This adaptability empowers organizations to innovate rapidly, expand confidently, and future-proof their technology investments in an ecosystem that continues to evolve.

Chapter 3

Predictive Analytics in Supply Chain Management

Predictive analytics has emerged as a powerful catalyst in reshaping the way supply chains function, shifting them from reactive networks to intelligent, forward-looking systems. With global markets becoming increasingly volatile and customer expectations evolving rapidly, businesses need more than historical data—they need predictive foresight. By leveraging machine learning models and real-time data feeds, predictive analytics enables organizations to anticipate demand fluctuations, mitigate risks, and streamline operations with a level of precision that was once unattainable.

At the core of predictive analytics lies the ability to harness structured and unstructured data to identify trends, anomalies, and future outcomes. Supply chains, which span complex networks of suppliers, manufacturers, logistics providers, and retailers, generate vast volumes of data daily. Predictive analytics sifts through this data to forecast key variables such as customer demand, inventory needs, transportation delays, and supplier reliability. These insights allow businesses to optimize procurement strategies, reduce waste, and maintain optimal stock levels improving efficiency while reducing operational costs.

The impact of predictive analytics extends across multiple layers of the supply chain. In procurement, predictive models can anticipate material shortages or price hikes, enabling smarter sourcing decisions. In logistics, route optimization tools use real-time and historical data to forecast delivery delays and suggest alternatives. In demand planning, algorithms analyze past purchasing behavior, seasonal trends, and external variables like weather or economic indicators to fine-tune inventory decisions. These applications work in tandem to build a supply chain that is not only responsive but proactive.

Beyond the tangible operational benefits, predictive analytics empowers decision-makers with confidence and clarity. Executives can simulate different scenarios such as supplier disruptions or spikes in consumer demand and evaluate their impact before acting. This capacity to "see around corners" is critical in a landscape where agility and adaptability define success. Predictive analytics transforms uncertainty into a competitive advantage, equipping organizations to prepare rather than merely react.

However, successful implementation requires more than technology. It demands cross-functional collaboration between data scientists, supply chain managers, IT professionals, and business leaders. Data governance, model accuracy, and continual learning loops must be maintained to ensure relevance and reliability. Organizations must also foster a culture of data-driven decision-making, where insights from predictive tools are actively embedded into daily operations and strategic planning.

Predictive analytics is not a singular tool but a shift in how supply chains are envisioned and operated. It marks a transition toward intelligent orchestration—where every node in the supply network is informed, aligned, and adaptable. As more organizations embrace this transformation, supply chains are no longer cost centers or risk zones. They become engines of strategic value, efficiency, and resilience in a world where adaptability is the new competitive edge.

Forecasting Demand and Reducing Uncertainty

Forecasting demand has long been a cornerstone of supply chain management, but the evolution of AI and predictive analytics has dramatically enhanced its accuracy and strategic importance. Traditional forecasting methods, largely reliant on historical sales data and linear projections, often fall short in today's fast-moving, data-saturated economy. Predictive analytics leverages machine learning models to uncover nuanced patterns and incorporate a broader range of variables, from economic indicators to social media sentiment, to improve forecasting precision.

This data-driven approach reduces uncertainty by enabling supply chain leaders to anticipate fluctuations in demand well before they occur. By identifying early signals of change—such as shifts in consumer behavior, regional disruptions, or emerging trends—organizations can better align production schedules, inventory levels, and logistics plans with anticipated needs. The result is a more responsive, cost-efficient operation that avoids the extremes of overstocking and stockouts.

Moreover, predictive demand forecasting empowers businesses to make proactive decisions. For example, a healthcare provider anticipating a surge in patient visits due to seasonal illnesses can pre-emptively secure critical medical supplies. Similarly, a retail chain expecting higher demand during a promotional campaign can optimize distribution to key outlets in advance. These anticipatory actions reduce delays, improve service delivery, and strengthen customer satisfaction.

Ultimately, forecasting powered by AI does more than reduce uncertainty it transforms it into opportunity. Organizations that can see and prepare for demand shifts ahead of time position themselves not just to survive disruptions but to outperform competitors through operational readiness and agility.

Inventory Optimization through Machine Learning

Effective inventory management is a defining factor in the efficiency and profitability of any supply chain. Traditional inventory systems often operate on static rules or fixed reorder points, which fail to adapt quickly to changing demand patterns or supply fluctuations. Machine learning introduces a dynamic, intelligent approach to inventory optimization—one that continuously learns from data, adjusts to new variables, and minimizes both excess and shortage.

By analyzing vast volumes of transactional data, seasonal trends, supplier performance metrics, and even external factors like weather or geopolitical shifts, machine learning models can predict the optimal stock levels required at different nodes of the supply chain. These models move beyond historical averages to identify subtle signals that influence inventory turnover, enabling organizations to maintain just the right amount of stock in real time.

This intelligence leads to reduced holding costs and fewer instances of obsolete inventory. For industries with perishable goods or high-value components, such optimization can significantly improve bottom-line results. In the pharmaceutical sector, for example, machine learning helps manage sensitive drug inventories with precision, reducing waste and ensuring availability where needed most.

Furthermore, machine learning supports continuous inventory health monitoring. Algorithms can flag slow-moving items, identify patterns in returns or stock-outs, and recommend replenishment strategies tailored to different regions or customer profiles. These insights enable supply chain leaders to make informed, agile decisions that align inventory practices with business goals and customer demand.

Incorporating machine learning into inventory management is not merely a tactical upgrade—it is a strategic shift. It positions organizations to be more responsive, efficient, and competitive in an environment where supply chain agility is critical for success.

Risk Assessment and Disruption Preparedness

In supply chain systems where the slightest disruption can ripple across networks and incur significant cost, predictive analytics provides a powerful lens for pre-empting risk and mitigating impact. At the core of disruption preparedness is the ability to assess risk dynamically, based not just on static historical data but on continuously evolving indicators drawn from internal operations and external variables.

By leveraging machine learning algorithms that learn from supply chain patterns, organizations can identify anomalies early such as sudden shifts in supplier reliability, regional instability, or transportation delays. These signals are converted into actionable insights, empowering supply chain managers to reroute shipments, adjust order volumes, or trigger contingency protocols well before a disruption materializes. The transformation from reactive to proactive strategy is one of the most valuable shifts predictive analytics enables.

Equally important is the integration of simulation environments, where various risk scenarios such as supplier failure, labour strikes, or inventory depletion are modelled to test system resilience. These simulations inform the development of playbooks for emergency response, ensuring that organizations are not caught unprepared. With data at the centre, risk no longer becomes a vague concern; it becomes a manageable element of strategic planning, allowing firms to maintain continuity, protect revenue, and strengthen stakeholder confidence.

Chapter 4

AI Driven Logistics and Last Mile Innovation

The transformation of logistics operations through artificial intelligence has reshaped the future of supply chain management, with last mile delivery emerging as a focal point of innovation. As businesses seek to meet rising customer expectations while managing operational costs, AI offers a strategic framework for intelligent logistics execution. Unlike earlier approaches that relied on rigid scheduling and static routing, AI introduces adaptability, data awareness, and learning capacity into every phase of movement.

AI driven logistics platforms enable real time decision making, allowing systems to adjust routes, delivery priorities, and resource allocation based on live conditions. This leads to significant improvements in speed, accuracy, and responsiveness. Particularly within the last mile—the most cost intensive and unpredictable segment of delivery AI empowers companies to better navigate dense urban networks, customer-specific constraints, and external disruptions. By learning from past data and anticipating future variables, AI ensures that logistics operations are not only faster but also smarter.

In essence, AI driven logistics and last mile innovation mark a shift from mechanical execution to intelligent coordination. The integration of learning systems into physical delivery processes creates a responsive and adaptive logistics environment. This evolution enables enterprises to reduce inefficiencies, enhance visibility, and deliver value precisely where it matters most: at the point of customer fulfilment.

Smart Routing and Transportation Optimization

Smart routing, powered by artificial intelligence, has emerged as a critical advancement in optimizing transportation networks. Traditional routing methods often relied on static data, manual input, and reactive planning, resulting in delays, increased fuel consumption, and higher operational costs. In contrast, AI-enabled routing systems leverage real-time data, historical trends, and predictive analytics to determine the most efficient paths for delivery fleets and supply movements.

These intelligent systems consider a multitude of variables—traffic patterns, weather conditions, vehicle performance, delivery windows, and even customer behavior—to generate dynamic routing recommendations. As the system continues to learn, it adapts to patterns and improves decision-making over time, reducing delivery time variability and enhancing service reliability. This shift toward predictive and adaptive routing reduces unnecessary mileage and carbon emissions, aligning business performance with sustainability goals.

The broader impact of smart routing extends beyond individual delivery events. It transforms transportation logistics into a proactive, cost-effective, and customer-responsive system. As more companies integrate AI into their transportation planning, the logistics sector gains new momentum

where precision, resilience, and strategic foresight define operational excellence.

Reducing Delivery Delays with Real-Time Models

Delivery delays represent one of the most persistent pain points in modern supply chains, particularly as customer expectations continue to trend toward immediacy and real-time fulfilment. Traditional logistics systems, often reliant on static routing and reactive scheduling, are poorly equipped to respond to dynamic conditions such as traffic fluctuations, sudden demand spikes, or last-minute route disruptions. Real-time AI models are now redefining how enterprises respond to these challenges

replacing guesswork with precision and latency with speed.

These models process a continuous stream of data from GPS trackers, warehouse sensors, traffic feeds, and customer orders to generate up-to-the-minute logistics decisions. By identifying bottlenecks as they arise, AI-powered systems can automatically reroute vehicles, adjust delivery priorities, or even redistribute inventory across distribution centers to meet changing demand. This real-time intelligence enables logistics managers to move from static scheduling to adaptive orchestration, reducing idle time and improving on-time delivery performance.

One of the most powerful outcomes of deploying real-time delivery models is the elevation of customer experience. Predictive alerts and live status tracking enable businesses to provide accurate ETAs and proactive notifications when delays are unavoidable. Such transparency builds trust and sets the foundation for customer retention in highly competitive markets. More importantly, it allows businesses to address small issues before they escalate, preserving service quality while optimizing operational efficiency.

In health supply chains, the impact is even more critical. Real-time delivery optimization has been deployed to ensure that life-saving medications and emergency medical equipment reach hospitals on time, especially in underserved or rural locations. These solutions combine historical delivery data with live updates to anticipate roadblocks, reroute deliveries, and prevent costly or dangerous delays. The ability to operate in real time turns logistics into a proactive system—where delivery windows are not just estimated but intelligently managed to achieve consistency and precision.

Ultimately, the integration of real-time AI models into last-mile logistics represents a shift from reactive operations to predictive control. By analyzing and responding to conditions as they unfold, organizations can eliminate inefficiencies, enhance performance metrics, and create a logistics network that is not only faster but also smarter. This transition reflects the core promise of AI in supply chain: creating systems that are resilient, responsive, and aligned with the speed of the modern economy.

Integrating AI with IoT in Logistics

Integrating Artificial Intelligence with the Internet of Things is revolutionizing logistics by creating intelligent, responsive, and self-optimizing supply chains. The synergy between AI and IoT allows logistics systems to gather real-time data from connected devices such as sensors, GPS trackers, and RFID tags, then process that data through AI models to enable faster and smarter decisions. This integration bridges the physical and digital layers of logistics, ensuring that operations remain synchronized, transparent, and adaptive at every stage.

At the operational level, IoT devices continuously collect data on shipment location, vehicle conditions, temperature, fuel consumption, and handling environments. When processed by AI, this stream of data translates into actionable insights. For instance, temperature-sensitive goods such as pharmaceuticals or perishable foods can be monitored for environmental changes, triggering AI-based interventions such as route alterations, dispatch adjustments, or condition-specific alerts. These dynamic responses help minimize spoilage, reduce wastage, and ensure compliance with safety standards.

AI-powered analytics further optimize how logistics network's function. Predictive maintenance models, fed by IoT sensor data, identify potential equipment failures before they occur, allowing organizations to schedule repairs and avoid costly downtime. AI also detects inefficiencies in delivery routes or warehouse operations, offering real-time suggestions for improvement. These optimizations reduce operating costs, improve delivery reliability, and increase overall system throughput without requiring manual intervention.

Moreover, integrating AI with IoT enhances supply chain visibility and security. With real-time tracking and anomaly detection, logistics managers can monitor cargo status across the entire journey. AI algorithms can flag inconsistencies such as unexpected stops, deviations from the route, or signs of tampering. This continuous surveillance builds accountability, reduces theft or fraud, and increases customer confidence by offering full transparency from origin to destination.

The convergence of AI and IoT in logistics is more than a technological upgrade; it is a strategic transformation. It empowers organizations to move from reactive logistics to anticipatory systems, capable of responding to changes before they disrupt operations. This level of intelligence not only improves efficiency but also creates a more agile and resilient logistics framework that supports long-term growth and adaptability in an increasingly complex global market.

Chapter 5

Natural Language Processing in Healthcare

Natural Language Processing has become a cornerstone of modern healthcare innovation, offering a transformative approach to how medical information is captured, analyzed, and utilized. As the healthcare sector increasingly digitizes, vast amounts of unstructured textual data ranging from clinical notes and patient records to diagnostic reports and treatment summaries remain underutilized. NLP bridges this gap by enabling machines to understand, interpret, and generate human language in ways that enhance care delivery, reduce administrative burden, and accelerate research.

One of the most impactful applications of NLP in healthcare is clinical documentation. Traditional methods of record-keeping often require healthcare professionals to spend hours inputting data manually, detracting from direct patient care. NLP-powered systems, however, can automate this process by transcribing and structuring physicians' notes in real-time. These tools extract relevant medical information such as symptoms, diagnoses, medications, and lab results, and convert them into standardized electronic formats. This not only improves accuracy and efficiency but also facilitates better interoperability between systems and providers.

NLP is also critical in unlocking insights from patient histories and identifying trends that might otherwise go unnoticed. Through semantic analysis, NLP tools can parse through thousands of records to detect commonalities in disease progression, treatment outcomes, or adverse drug reactions. These capabilities enhance clinical decision support systems by offering timely recommendations, risk stratification, and evidence-based treatment options tailored to individual patients. In fields like oncology, cardiology, and mental health, NLP contributes to more precise diagnoses and personalized care strategies.

In research and public health, NLP supports large-scale analysis of population health data, epidemiological studies, and health surveillance. By analyzing medical literature, social media, and health forums, NLP can identify emerging disease patterns or gauge patient sentiment toward healthcare services. This information enables governments, hospitals, and policy makers to respond quickly to health crises and to refine healthcare delivery models based on real-world feedback.

The integration of NLP into healthcare marks a shift toward more intelligent, responsive, and patient-centered systems. By translating unstructured data into actionable intelligence, NLP not only improves operational efficiency but also enhances the overall quality of care. As the healthcare industry continues to evolve, the role of NLP will expand paving the way for innovations that align clinical precision with empathetic, data-driven medicine.

Automating Clinical Documentation

Clinical documentation has long been one of the most time-consuming tasks for healthcare professionals. For decades, physicians, nurses, and clinical support teams have invested hours in recording patient encounters, transcribing notes, and updating electronic health records. While this process is essential to care delivery, it has traditionally placed a significant strain on both time and accuracy. Natural Language Processing (NLP), a critical branch of artificial intelligence, is now offering a profound solution: automating the entire documentation workflow to ensure precision, efficiency, and better clinical outcomes.

The application of NLP in automating clinical documentation begins with its ability to understand and interpret human language—spoken or written—in medical contexts. During consultations, AI-powered voice recognition tools integrated with NLP engines listen in real time, converting conversations between patients and providers into structured clinical entries. This transformation is more than transcription. The system identifies, extracts, and categorizes relevant information such as symptoms, diagnoses, allergies, prescriptions, and follow-up instructions. These data points are then accurately mapped to standardized coding systems such as SNOMED CT or ICD-10, ensuring interoperability and compliance across health information systems.

Automated clinical documentation is not simply about speed it is about consistency and cognitive offloading. Clinicians no longer need to rely on memory or hand-written notes after appointments. Instead, the information is captured accurately as it happens. This not only enhances clinical productivity but also reduces errors caused by misinterpretation, illegible notes, or forgotten details. Moreover, because the system is designed to learn over time, it becomes increasingly adept at recognizing context, detecting rare terminologies, and adjusting to specialty-specific language, thereby becoming a trusted partner in complex care environments.

Patient safety also benefits significantly from NLP automation. Accurate documentation ensures that treatment decisions are based on complete and up-to-date records. For example, medication reconciliation a critical process to avoid harmful drug interactions—relies heavily on precise patient histories. NLP systems can instantly compare new prescriptions with existing medication records and flag potential risks. In emergency or high-pressure settings, this real-time alerting capability can make a life-saving difference.

Beyond the bedside, automated clinical documentation is changing how data flows through administrative systems. Billing departments, insurance claims processors, and medical coders can access structured, validated records without repeated manual intervention. This not only accelerates revenue cycle management but also reduces claim denials and legal disputes stemming from incomplete or inconsistent documentation. Hospitals and healthcare systems benefit from improved audit readiness, greater transparency, and more reliable performance metrics.

Furthermore, automated documentation strengthens the doctor–patient relationship. With less time spent typing into computers, clinicians can be more present, listening deeply and responding empathetically. Many patients report greater satisfaction when they feel seen and heard, without the intrusion of constant notetaking. As NLP continues to mature, it holds the promise of restoring the human connection at the heart of healthcare while enhancing precision and operational efficiency behind the scenes.

Ultimately, automating clinical documentation through NLP is a transformative advancement in healthcare delivery. It integrates the power of artificial intelligence with the nuances of medical practice, producing systems that are not only intelligent but also context-aware, compliant, and user-centric. As adoption grows, these technologies will become foundational in the digital transformation of hospitals, clinics, and health networks worldwide—freeing clinicians to focus on what matters most: patient care.

Improving Diagnostic Accuracy with NLP

Natural Language Processing is redefining the way healthcare professionals interpret and act upon clinical data, particularly in the domain of diagnostics. By enabling machines to comprehend and process unstructured clinical narratives such as patient histories, radiology reports, physician notes, and pathology results NLP reduces the manual burden on medical personnel and significantly improves diagnostic efficiency. Traditionally, vital information buried within free-text documents could go unnoticed or be inconsistently interpreted, resulting in diagnostic delays or oversight. NLP tools extract key entities, patterns, and contextual relationships that are relevant for accurate and timely diagnosis, ensuring that no important detail is missed.

Beyond data extraction, NLP systems are capable of synthesizing knowledge across multiple documents and sources. This is especially beneficial when diagnosing complex or rare conditions that require a holistic view of a patient's medical history. For example, NLP algorithms can identify recurring symptoms across past reports, flag medication conflicts, or even suggest potential diagnoses based on aggregated textual data, complementing the physician's decision-making process. This layered insight offers a more nuanced, data-enriched diagnostic approach.

Moreover, integrating NLP into electronic health record systems allows for real-time feedback and alerts that guide clinicians toward more precise treatment paths. Machine learning models trained on vast clinical corpora continue to refine their understanding, reducing false positives and improving sensitivity. By aligning linguistic comprehension with clinical protocols, NLP-driven solutions support faster, safer, and more accurate diagnoses, ultimately improving patient outcomes across healthcare systems.

Enhancing Physician Decision Support Systems

Enhancing physician decision support systems with Natural Language Processing has become a transformative advancement in modern healthcare. These systems are designed to assist clinicians in making timely, evidence-based decisions by offering relevant insights extracted from large volumes of unstructured data. Through NLP, medical notes, discharge summaries, and research literature are analyzed in real time to surface key information that would otherwise require hours of manual review. This immediate access to contextually relevant data ensures that physicians are equipped with a comprehensive understanding of a patient's condition, supporting better clinical judgment.

NLP also allows decision support systems to interpret patient data within the broader scope of medical guidelines and current research. For instance, an NLP-powered system can cross-reference a patient's symptoms and history with the latest treatment protocols or identify potential contraindications based on medication history. This dynamic analysis not only streamlines clinical workflows but also reduces the likelihood of diagnostic and therapeutic errors. It functions as a silent partner in the diagnostic room—offering suggestions, alerting to discrepancies, and reinforcing clinical best practices.

Furthermore, by integrating NLP with electronic health records and clinical databases, decision support systems continuously evolve and adapt to institutional needs. They begin to recognize organizational patterns, physician preferences, and patient demographics, offering tailored support that reflects local realities. This contextual awareness enhances both the relevance and accuracy of recommendations, ensuring that the technology augments rather than interrupts the clinical process. Ultimately,

NLP-enhanced decision support helps deliver more personalized, efficient, and reliable care in increasingly complex healthcare environments.

Chapter 6

Deep Learning for Medical Imaging and Diagnostics

Deep learning has emerged as a transformative force in the field of medical imaging and diagnostics. By enabling machines to process vast volumes of visual data with accuracy that often rivals or surpasses human experts, deep learning algorithms are redefining how diseases are detected, classified, and monitored. From radiology and pathology to ophthalmology and oncology, artificial neural networks are being trained to analyze complex medical images and provide actionable insights that support early diagnosis, treatment planning, and outcome prediction.

Medical imaging is central to modern healthcare. Whether through X-rays, MRIs, CT scans, or ultrasound, images provide critical visual cues that guide clinical decision-making. Traditionally, interpreting these images has required skilled radiologists, who painstakingly review each scan to identify anomalies. However, the growing demand for imaging services, coupled with workforce shortages in many regions, has created gaps in timely diagnostics. Deep learning addresses this challenge by automating image analysis. Convolutional neural networks (CNNs) have shown exceptional capability in detecting patterns and anomalies, learning from thousands of labelled images to differentiate between healthy and abnormal tissue.

One of the key advantages of deep learning in this domain is its ability to process high-dimensional data. Medical images are rich in detail, and subtle features often imperceptible to the human eye—can carry significant diagnostic value. Deep learning models trained on diverse datasets can identify these minute patterns and make probabilistic inferences about the presence of disease. For instance, deep learning has demonstrated remarkable accuracy in identifying early-stage breast cancer from mammograms and spotting diabetic retinopathy in retinal scans. In many of these applications, the models not only flag potential abnormalities but also provide visual explanations (e.g., heatmaps) that enhance clinician trust and transparency.

Another area where deep learning is making an impact is pathology. Whole-slide imaging (WSI) has revolutionized how tissue samples are digitized and analyzed. With gigapixel-scale pathology images, manual review is both time-consuming and prone to subjectivity. Deep learning enables automated scanning of tissue slides, detecting cellular-level changes indicative of cancer, inflammation, or degenerative diseases. These capabilities support pathologists by acting as a second set of eyes—highlighting areas of concern, prioritizing cases, and improving diagnostic throughput. Moreover, combining histopathological data with clinical and genomic information further elevates predictive accuracy.

Despite the impressive results, the deployment of deep learning in medical imaging must navigate several challenges. Model generalization across different populations, imaging devices, and clinical settings remains a concern. Biases in training data can affect model performance, potentially leading to health disparities if not properly addressed. Additionally, regulatory approval, data privacy, and model explainability are critical considerations. Regulatory bodies like the FDA have begun establishing frameworks for evaluating AI-based diagnostic tools, ensuring safety, efficacy, and fairness.

Ultimately, deep learning is not meant to replace clinicians but to augment their capabilities. It functions as a powerful assistant, reducing diagnostic workload, increasing consistency, and enabling faster decision-making. As models continue to evolve and integrate seamlessly with electronic medical records and clinical workflows, their role in diagnostics will become even more indispensable. For healthcare systems aiming to scale services, reduce errors, and improve patient outcomes, the strategic adoption of deep learning in medical imaging is not just an innovation it is a necessity.

Image Recognition in Radiology and Pathology

The integration of image recognition powered by deep learning has significantly advanced both radiology and pathology, offering new dimensions of precision, efficiency, and scale in diagnostics. Radiology, long reliant on expert human interpretation of X-rays, CT scans, and MRIs, is now experiencing a paradigm shift where intelligent systems assist in reviewing and interpreting images at unprecedented speed and accuracy. Similarly, pathology, which involves the microscopic examination of tissues and cells, benefits immensely from algorithms capable of detecting minute structural abnormalities that signal disease progression or malignancy.

In radiology, convolutional neural networks (CNNs) have demonstrated exceptional capability in classifying medical images and identifying a range of conditions, from fractures and tumours to pulmonary nodules and neurological abnormalities. These models are trained on extensive datasets containing thousands of labelled images, allowing them to learn the visual patterns associated with specific diseases. Once deployed, they can analyze new radiographs within seconds, flagging suspicious regions for further review by radiologists. This capability enhances diagnostic throughput and reduces the likelihood of missed findings, especially in time-critical or resource-constrained environments.

Pathology has traditionally been limited by manual slide review, a process that is labour-intensive and susceptible to human variability. Digital pathology, combined with image recognition models, transforms this process by enabling automated analysis of high-resolution whole-slide images. Deep learning algorithms can be trained to identify features such as mitotic figures, nuclear pleomorphism, tissue architecture, and other histopathological markers that are often associated with cancer, autoimmune disorders, or infectious diseases. These tools not only reduce the burden on pathologists but also standardize assessments and improve the reproducibility of diagnoses across institutions.

One of the most powerful outcomes of image recognition in these fields is the ability to enable early detection and longitudinal monitoring of disease. For example, AI-powered radiology systems can compare scans over time to identify subtle changes that may not yet be clinically apparent, thus facilitating earlier intervention. In pathology, models can quantify biomarkers and morphometric data, contributing to personalized treatment plans by linking tissue features with therapeutic response patterns. Such granular analysis was previously difficult to scale manually but is now feasible with machine intelligence.

Despite these advancements, clinical adoption requires cautious implementation. Image recognition models must be validated across diverse patient populations, imaging modalities, and clinical environments to ensure robustness and avoid algorithmic bias. Additionally, regulatory bodies mandate rigorous testing and explainability to confirm that decisions made by AI systems are transparent and reliable. Integrating these tools into existing clinical workflows also demands thoughtful design to ensure they support rather than disrupt medical practice.

As image recognition in radiology and pathology continues to evolve, it holds the potential to democratize access to expert-level diagnostics, particularly in underserved regions with limited specialist availability. By acting as force multipliers, these technologies empower clinicians to make faster, more informed decisions, ultimately improving outcomes and expanding the reach of high-quality care.

Data Labelling, Training, and Validation Challenges

In the development of deep learning models for medical imaging and diagnostics, the quality and integrity of training data are foundational to performance. Among the most critical and complex components of this process are data labelling, model training, and validation—each of which introduces unique technical, ethical, and logistical challenges. As artificial intelligence continues to drive breakthroughs in radiology, pathology, and other diagnostic domains, understanding and addressing these challenges becomes essential to ensure the reliability and clinical utility of AI-powered systems.

Data labelling in medical imaging is particularly demanding because it requires precise annotations from domain experts such as radiologists or pathologists. Unlike general image recognition tasks where labels like "dog" or "car" can be easily assigned, medical images demand highly granular labels such as tumour boundaries, lesion types, or grades of abnormality. These annotations must be accurate, consistent, and clinically relevant, as they form the basis for how the algorithm learns to detect similar features in new data. Unfortunately, expert annotation is time-consuming and expensive, limiting the volume of labelled datasets available for training. Moreover, inter-observer variability among clinicians can introduce inconsistencies that affect model generalizability.

The training phase poses its own set of obstacles. Deep learning models are inherently data-hungry and require large volumes of high-quality, diverse data to avoid overfitting and to perform well in real-world scenarios. In medical imaging, acquiring such data is complicated by privacy regulations, disparate imaging standards, and unequal representation of diseases across populations. For example, a model trained predominantly on data from one demographic or imaging centre may not perform well when deployed in a different context. Addressing this challenge often requires pooling data across multiple institutions, which brings up concerns about data sharing agreements, interoperability, and compliance with healthcare regulations such as HIPAA or GDPR.

Validation is the third critical pillar and serves as the final gatekeeper before clinical deployment. Effective validation requires testing the model on datasets that were not used during training, ideally from different institutions or patient populations. This step helps to assess the model's robustness and ability to generalize across varied conditions. However, many early-stage studies rely on internal validation, which may inflate performance metrics and obscure real-world limitations. Furthermore, because clinical decision-making has high stakes, validation protocols must align with rigorous standards comparable to those used for traditional medical devices. This includes sensitivity and specificity analysis, comparison with human expert performance, and assessment of the model's interpretability and consistency.

Another challenge across all three phases is the handling of edge cases and rare conditions. In medicine, these instances are often underrepresented in datasets but critically important for diagnosis. Training data that lacks sufficient examples of rare diseases or atypical presentations may lead to models that are accurate in common scenarios but fail during outlier cases. To mitigate this, researchers often employ techniques such as data augmentation, synthetic data generation, and active learning, but each comes with trade-offs that must be carefully considered.

In summary, building trustworthy AI models for medical imaging requires meticulous attention to data labeling, thoughtful training strategies, and comprehensive validation. These processes must be guided not just by technical acumen but by close collaboration with clinicians, ethicists, and regulatory experts. By navigating these challenges responsibly, developers can create diagnostic tools that are not only powerful but also equitable, transparent, and ready for real-world healthcare delivery.

Real Time Decision Making in Emergency Care

The application of artificial intelligence to real time decision making in emergency care is one of the most transformative intersections of technology and medicine. Emergency departments operate in high pressure environments where rapid assessment and timely intervention can mean the difference between life and death. The integration of AI systems in these settings aims to enhance triage accuracy, streamline diagnostic processes, and support critical decisions with data driven precision. These systems do not replace the expertise of emergency physicians but rather serve as intelligent collaborators, offering rapid insights derived from vast datasets and learned patterns.

One of the most promising uses of AI in emergency care is the triage process. Traditional triage relies on protocols and the clinical judgment of nurses or attending physicians, often under high stress and with limited data at hand. AI systems, particularly those powered by machine learning, can analyze patient symptoms, vital signs, and historical data to recommend priority levels for treatment. These tools can rapidly sift through electronic health records, flag potential complications, and provide predictive risk scores. This support helps clinicians allocate resources more efficiently, ensuring that patients with critical needs receive immediate attention while reducing delays for others.

AI also plays a growing role in diagnostic assistance, especially when time is of the essence. For example, in cases of suspected stroke or trauma, deep learning models can rapidly analyze imaging results and detect abnormalities that may not be immediately visible to the human eye. These insights are delivered in seconds, enabling physicians to make informed decisions about interventions such as thrombolysis or surgery. In cardiac emergencies, AI systems connected to real time monitoring devices can detect early signs of arrhythmia, myocardial infarction, or cardiac arrest, prompting clinicians to intervene before the situation escalates.

Real time AI support is also being deployed through natural language processing, which allows systems to extract relevant clinical notes and context from unstructured data in medical records. This capability is crucial in emergency care, where patients may be unconscious or unable to communicate clearly. AI can help summarize previous diagnoses, medications, allergies, and recent test results, presenting a clear clinical picture to the attending team within moments. This not only aids in accurate decision making but also minimizes the cognitive burden on physicians who must process large amounts of information quickly.

Challenges remain, particularly in ensuring that AI systems are reliable and fair under all conditions. The urgency of emergency care means that any AI tool must be tested for robustness and resilience under stress. Additionally, real time systems must be designed to integrate seamlessly with existing clinical workflows, minimizing disruption rather than adding complexity. Human oversight is essential to ensure that AI recommendations are interpreted correctly and contextualized within each unique patient scenario.

Ultimately, the goal of AI in emergency care is to enhance speed, accuracy, and patient outcomes. By supporting clinicians with intelligent, real-time insights, AI enables a new standard of responsive care that balances urgency with precision. As these systems continue to evolve, they hold the promise of transforming emergency medicine from reactive treatment to proactive, data enriched decision making—saving lives and improving efficiency in one of healthcare's most critical frontlines.

Chapter 7

Fraud Detection and Risk Analytics in Finance

In the modern financial ecosystem, the sophistication of fraudulent schemes has grown exponentially alongside digital transformation. Traditional rule-based systems, once the cornerstone of fraud prevention, are now insufficient to detect evolving threats that exploit system vulnerabilities in nuanced ways. Artificial intelligence, particularly when paired with robust risk analytics, has emerged as a powerful tool in safeguarding financial integrity. In this chapter, we explore how AI enables real-time fraud detection, supports adaptive risk modelling, and transforms financial security across banking, payments, insurance, and capital markets.

AI-powered fraud detection systems excel at identifying subtle patterns and anomalies across massive transaction datasets. Unlike static models that depend on predefined rules, machine learning algorithms learn from historical fraud cases, continuously improving their detection capabilities as new data becomes available. These systems use supervised learning to classify fraudulent and legitimate transactions based on labelled datasets and unsupervised learning to identify novel fraud patterns by recognizing outliers that deviate from standard customer behavior. This flexibility allows institutions to detect not only known fraud schemes but also emerging threats in real time.

Financial institutions are also leveraging deep learning models for behavioural profiling. By analyzing variables such as device usage, transaction time, frequency, location, and spending habits, AI can generate dynamic risk scores for each transaction. If a transaction diverges significantly from a customer's normal behavior—say, a sudden withdrawal in a foreign country or a large purchase made at an odd hour—the system can flag the activity for manual review or automatically trigger verification protocols. This adaptive learning approach helps reduce false positives, which are common in traditional fraud systems and often result in poor customer experience.

Risk analytics in finance goes beyond fraud detection; it encompasses credit risk assessment, market risk modelling, and operational risk management. Predictive analytics tools allow financial institutions to evaluate a borrower's likelihood of default by considering a wide range of structured and unstructured data, including transaction history, employment patterns, and even sentiment analysis from public records or social media. In capital markets, AI models simulate thousands of scenarios using historical data to stress test investment portfolios under varied economic conditions. This proactive approach equips institutions with foresight and agility in responding to potential market shocks.

In the realm of insurance, AI contributes to fraud prevention through automated claims processing and anomaly detection. By cross-checking claims with historical data, AI systems can identify inconsistencies that suggest fabrication or exaggeration. For example, if a policyholder has submitted multiple similar claims across different insurers, or if the claim contradicts public data sources such as accident reports, the system can flag it for deeper investigation. Such capabilities not only protect the insurer but also help maintain fair pricing and trust in the industry.

While the benefits of AI in fraud detection and risk analytics are substantial, implementation is not without challenges. Ensuring data privacy, maintaining model transparency, and avoiding algorithmic bias are critical. Financial institutions must adopt explainable AI frameworks that allow regulators and stakeholders to understand how decisions are made. Moreover, continuous monitoring is required to detect data drift and ensure that models remain effective in the face of changing fraud tactics and economic conditions.

As financial operations continue to digitize, AI will become not just a security enhancement but a strategic enabler. Its ability to provide real-time insights, dynamic adaptation, and predictive foresight makes it indispensable in the fight against fraud and in managing financial risk. Institutions that harness these tools effectively will not only mitigate threats but also build resilient, data-driven financial ecosystems capable of supporting sustainable growth in an increasingly volatile environment.

Anomaly Detection with Supervised Learning

Anomaly detection plays a pivotal role in identifying fraudulent activity and operational risks within financial systems. In supervised learning, this technique relies on labeled datasets that classify previous transactions or events as either normal or anomalous. The goal is to train a machine learning model that can accurately distinguish between legitimate and fraudulent behaviors based on patterns learned from historical data. This approach is particularly effective in environments where known fraud types are well documented and can be used to teach the model what to look for.

The process begins with the collection of high-quality, annotated data—each transaction or financial event is marked as either legitimate or fraudulent. Common features used in training models include transaction amount, location, frequency, device type, and user behavior over time. Supervised learning algorithms such as decision trees, logistic regression, support vector machines, and neural networks are then employed to develop a predictive model. These models learn the correlations between input features and the target variable (fraud or no fraud), enabling them to assign probabilities to new, unseen data.

Once deployed, the model scans incoming data streams in real time, evaluating each instance against its learned parameters. When the model identifies characteristics that closely resemble known fraudulent patterns, it raises an alert for further investigation. For example, a sudden, high-value international transfer from a dormant account might be flagged immediately. The strength of supervised learning lies in its precision—given quality training data, it can achieve high accuracy and reduce false positives, which is crucial in maintaining customer trust and operational efficiency.

However, the effectiveness of supervised anomaly detection hinges on the availability and balance of labeled data. Fraudulent cases often represent a small fraction of total transactions, leading to class imbalance problems that can skew model performance. To address this, techniques such as oversampling of minority classes, under-sampling of majority classes, or using ensemble models like random forests can be employed to boost accuracy. Moreover, regular retraining is necessary to keep the model updated with evolving fraud tactics.

Supervised learning models for anomaly detection are increasingly being integrated into broader risk management systems, providing financial institutions with an intelligent layer of defense. By combining speed, accuracy, and adaptability, these models not only detect threats but also empower institutions to respond swiftly and strategically to financial anomalies.

Reducing False Positives with Deep Models

One of the persistent challenges in fraud detection and financial risk analytics is the high rate of false positives. These occur when legitimate transactions are incorrectly flagged as fraudulent, leading to customer dissatisfaction, operational bottlenecks, and unnecessary investigation costs. Deep learning models offer a robust approach to addressing this issue by improving pattern recognition, contextual understanding, and overall predictive accuracy.

Traditional models like logistic regression or decision trees may rely on a limited set of features and simple decision boundaries, making them more prone to misclassification in complex or ambiguous scenarios. In contrast, deep models such as convolutional neural networks (CNNs), recurrent neural networks (RNNs), and deep feedforward networks are capable of learning intricate patterns and latent representations from large volumes of structured and unstructured financial data. This includes transaction metadata, user behavior logs, device fingerprints, and even textual descriptions.

By leveraging multiple layers of abstraction, deep learning models can identify subtle and non-linear relationships that are typically missed by shallow models. For example, an RNN trained on sequential transaction data can learn behavioral patterns specific to individual users or accounts, making it easier to spot deviations that genuinely suggest fraud while ignoring rare but legitimate actions. This leads to a significant reduction in false positive rates, especially when models are fine-tuned with user-level or segment-level contextual information.

Another advantage of deep models is their ability to incorporate attention mechanisms and feature embeddings that allow the system to weigh the importance of different input features dynamically. These techniques help in distinguishing between noise and signals, especially in environments where financial behavior can vary widely across users or time periods. When deployed alongside real-time scoring engines, these models continuously update their understanding of what constitutes normal behavior, adapting to shifts in user patterns without rigid rules.

Moreover, integrating deep models with feedback loops—where results from human investigation teams are fed back into the system—creates a continuous learning environment. This allows the model to refine its classifications based on outcomes, thereby reducing the likelihood of repeating the same misclassifications. Institutions often combine deep models with explainable AI (XAI) techniques to provide interpretable justifications for flagged transactions, further increasing trust in the model's decisions.

Ultimately, the use of deep models in reducing false positives is not just about minimizing errors—it is about enhancing operational efficiency and customer satisfaction. By ensuring that fraud detection systems are both sensitive and specific, financial institutions can maintain tighter security controls while preserving a smooth and trustworthy experience for legitimate users.

Real-Time Monitoring for Secure Transactions

In an era of increasing digital financial activity, real-time monitoring has emerged as a critical component for ensuring the security and integrity of financial transactions. The speed at which fraudulent behavior can occur necessitates systems that are not only reactive but also proactive capable of identifying and responding to suspicious activities the moment they occur. Artificial intelligence, particularly when powered by deep learning and advanced analytics, provides the framework for such instantaneous oversight.

Real-time monitoring systems utilize streams of transactional data, customer behavior logs, device identifiers, geolocation signals, and contextual metadata to construct a dynamic, real-world view of financial operations. These systems process thousands of data points per second and employ machine learning algorithms that continuously assess risk in the background. The goal is to identify patterns or anomalies that deviate from an established baseline of normal behavior, without interrupting the user experience for legitimate customers.

AI models such as recurrent neural networks (RNNs) and attention-based transformers are particularly effective in tracking sequential data, such as the flow of payments, login attempts, or withdrawal sequences. They learn to anticipate expected patterns and can flag sudden or subtle deviations that might indicate account takeovers, synthetic identity usage, or coordinated fraud rings. By applying these techniques in real time, institutions can prevent financial loss before it occurs, as opposed to relying solely on retrospective analysis.

Moreover, real-time AI-powered monitoring systems are adaptable. As fraudsters evolve their techniques—deploying bots, mimicking user behavior, or exploiting systemic vulnerabilities—AI models can be retrained and reinforced with fresh data. This adaptability ensures resilience in rapidly shifting threat environments. Importantly, these systems can be paired with tiered alert mechanisms that escalate critical issues immediately, route lower-confidence flags for human review, and auto-resolve low-risk actions, thereby maintaining balance between security and operational efficiency.

Financial institutions are also integrating explainable AI (XAI) into their real-time monitoring platforms, offering transparency into why a transaction was flagged or blocked. This is crucial for compliance, auditing, and customer trust. Customers who are falsely flagged are more likely to accept disruptions when there is clarity and recourse, while regulatory bodies demand a clear rationale for all decisions, especially in markets with strict financial oversight.

Ultimately, real-time monitoring systems driven by AI are transforming the way financial institutions approach security. Rather than treating fraud as an isolated event to be investigated post-facto, these intelligent systems treat every transaction as part of an evolving behavioral context. The result is a proactive, adaptive, and highly responsive defense mechanism that strengthens trust and keeps digital financial ecosystems both agile and secure.

Chapter 8

Cross-Functional Collaboration in AI Projects

The success of artificial intelligence projects in complex industries does not rely solely on algorithms or data it hinges on the strength of collaboration across disciplines. AI solutions, by their nature, are multifaceted and require the integration of diverse knowledge systems: data science, domain expertise, engineering, compliance, business strategy, and user experience. Without effective cross-functional collaboration, even the most advanced models' risk being misaligned with operational goals or failing to deliver measurable value.

In AI-powered environments such as healthcare, finance, and supply chain, teams must co-create at every stage of development—from problem definition to deployment. For example, a data scientist working on predictive maintenance for a logistics network must work alongside supply chain managers who understand asset behavior, field engineers who deal with real-time operational challenges, and financial analysts who track cost implications. Each stakeholder brings a unique lens, and their insights help refine models to be both accurate and actionable.

This type of collaboration calls for a shared language and mutual respect between functions. Data scientists must learn to explain complex models without jargon, while business leaders must develop foundational AI literacy to make informed decisions. Project managers play a pivotal role as translators and integrators—mapping timelines, aligning incentives, and ensuring that contributions are harmonized toward a unified objective. Teams that succeed are those who build trust, navigate ambiguity together, and prioritize collective intelligence over siloed expertise.

Technology tools also play an enabling role. Agile frameworks, project management platforms, collaborative code repositories, and shared data environments foster real-time interaction and accountability. However, tools are only as powerful as the culture that uses them. High-functioning AI teams invest in psychological safety, inclusiveness, and regular retrospectives to refine both their processes and interpersonal dynamics. This creates an environment where innovation thrives, and failures become learning opportunities rather than setbacks.

Organizational leadership must also evolve. Traditional hierarchies are often too rigid for the iterative, exploratory nature of AI work. Instead, dynamic team structures that flex based on project phases are more effective. Leadership should champion cross-functional efforts, incentivize knowledge sharing, and recognize collaborative success as much as individual brilliance. In doing so, they signal that AI is not the domain of a few, but a collective effort that belongs to the entire organization.

Ultimately, cross-functional collaboration is not merely a best practice it is a necessity. In high-stakes industries, AI initiatives influence critical outcomes: patient health, financial security, product delivery, and public safety. When professionals from varied backgrounds unite under a shared mission, guided by structured collaboration and open communication, AI becomes more than a tool—it becomes a force for sustainable, inclusive, and transformational change.

Aligning Technical Goals with Business Strategy

In the rapidly evolving landscape of artificial intelligence, one of the most critical success factors for AI-driven projects is the alignment of technical objectives with broader business strategy. Organizations that treat AI as a siloed technical initiative often struggle to realize its full value. Conversely, when AI development is closely integrated with strategic priorities—such as improving customer experience, reducing operational costs, or enabling new revenue models—the impact is both measurable and sustained.

Aligning technical goals with business strategy begins with clarity at the top. Executives and business leaders must articulate the specific outcomes they seek from AI adoption. These could range from automating repetitive processes and improving forecast accuracy to uncovering hidden insights from unstructured data. Once these goals are defined, they serve as a compass for data scientists and engineers, who can design models and systems that address these targets directly, avoiding the common trap of building technically sophisticated solutions that solve the wrong problems.

A critical component of this alignment is effective communication between technical teams and business stakeholders. Technical professionals must be able to translate model performance metrics into language that resonates with business value. For example, a model's precision and recall are important, but explaining how these metrics reduce customer churn or prevent fraud makes their significance clear to decision-makers. On the other hand, business leaders must gain enough AI literacy to understand the possibilities and limitations of the technology, ensuring that expectations are both ambitious and grounded.

Cross-functional alignment also ensures efficient resource allocation. When technical goals mirror business imperatives, organizations avoid wasting time on low-impact initiatives. Instead, teams can prioritize projects that deliver strategic value—such as AI systems that enhance supply chain agility, improve diagnostic accuracy in healthcare, or increase transparency in financial transactions. This focus not only accelerates return on investment but also reinforces stakeholder trust in AI initiatives.

Furthermore, this alignment fosters long-term sustainability. AI systems must evolve as business conditions change. By embedding technical development within strategic planning cycles, organizations ensure that their AI capabilities remain adaptive and relevant. This dynamic integration supports continuous innovation while maintaining strategic cohesion, allowing businesses to remain competitive in volatile markets.

Ultimately, aligning technical goals with business strategy transforms AI from a set of isolated experiments into a central pillar of enterprise success. It bridges the gap between innovation and execution, ensuring that data science efforts drive outcomes that matter most. Through intentional collaboration, shared understanding, and mutual accountability, organizations can build AI systems that do not just operate efficiently but contribute meaningfully to growth, resilience, and strategic advantage.

Managing Multi-Disciplinary AI Teams

Building effective AI solutions requires more than just advanced algorithms or powerful computational tools—it demands cohesive, multi-disciplinary collaboration. Managing diverse teams made up of data scientists, software engineers, domain experts, product managers, and business stakeholders is both a strategic challenge and an operational necessity. Each contributor brings unique perspectives, skill sets, and priorities, and the ability to harmonize these differences often determines the success or failure of AI initiatives.

At the core of managing multi-disciplinary AI teams is the establishment of a shared language. While data scientists might discuss model interpretability or overfitting, business leaders focus on key performance indicators and return on investment. Healthcare professionals may prioritize patient safety, while supply chain experts emphasize efficiency and delivery timelines. The team lead must ensure that everyone understands the overarching goals of the project and how their individual contributions fit into that bigger picture. Creating forums for regular dialogue, such as sprint reviews or cross-functional check-ins, helps to bridge these linguistic and conceptual gaps.

Another critical factor is role clarity. In AI projects, overlapping responsibilities can lead to confusion, redundancy, or gaps in execution. For example, without clearly defined roles, there may be misalignment over who curates training data, who evaluates model performance, or who ensures compliance with regulatory standards. Defining each team member's scope of work and how they will interact with others promotes accountability and smoother workflows. Leaders must be intentional in assigning responsibilities and ensuring that technical and non-technical tasks are evenly distributed.

Effective management also involves creating an environment that encourages psychological safety and mutual respect. In multi-disciplinary teams, it is common for individuals to come from vastly different backgrounds engineering, medicine, logistics, finance, and beyond. Encouraging open communication, where team members feel comfortable expressing uncertainty or raising concerns, fosters creativity and problem-solving. When experts from different disciplines collaborate without fear of judgment, they are more likely to uncover novel insights and arrive at robust, well-rounded solutions.

Moreover, successful AI team management involves resolving friction that may arise from differences in work pace or decision-making styles. Engineers may prefer rapid iteration, while domain experts may require extensive validation. Reconciling these dynamics calls for empathetic leadership and adaptive planning. Leaders must ensure that the team's structure is flexible enough to accommodate the varying rhythms of work while staying aligned with project timelines.

Finally, managing a multi-disciplinary AI team is also about continuous learning. As AI continues to evolve, so do the demands on those who work within it. Encouraging professional development across technical and domain disciplines ensures that the team remains competitive and capable of tackling emerging challenges. Whether through training sessions, cross-team shadowing, or collaborative workshops, fostering a culture of growth and curiosity enables the team to innovate effectively and deliver impact.

Managing multi-disciplinary AI teams is an exercise in integration—of people, expertise, and purpose. When led with clarity, respect, and vision, such teams become engines of transformation, capable of solving complex problems and delivering solutions that are as functional as they are strategic.

Communicating Insights to Non-Technical Stakeholders

One of the most critical skills in AI project execution is the ability to translate complex technical outcomes into meaningful, actionable insights for non-technical stakeholders. Data scientists and engineers often operate in a world of models, algorithms, confidence intervals, and performance metrics, but these concepts may be unfamiliar or even intimidating to decision-makers in business, healthcare, or finance. The real value of AI emerges when those insights are understood clearly enough to drive decisions, influence strategy, and inspire action.

To begin, effective communication starts with empathy understanding the audience's priorities, language, and level of familiarity with technology. Business leaders, for example, may care less about how a predictive model was trained and more about how it can reduce operational costs or increase customer retention. Clinicians want to know how an NLP system improves patient documentation or enhances diagnostic accuracy, not the specifics of tokenization or sequence modelling. Translating results into terms aligned with stakeholder concerns helps bridge the gap between technical complexity and business relevance.

Visualization plays a central role in this translation process. Charts, dashboards, and interactive reports can condense vast amounts of data into intuitive visuals that reveal trends, anomalies, and key patterns. Tools like confusion matrices, ROC curves, or time-series forecasts are useful for technical teams but may require simplification or alternative formats such as KPI-based performance summaries or cost-benefit simulations when presenting to executive leadership. The goal is to show the "so what" behind the "how," offering clarity without oversimplification.

Narrative framing is equally important. Storytelling can contextualize data insights by aligning them with real-world scenarios, user experiences, or strategic goals. A well-crafted narrative explains the problem, highlights the AI solution, presents the outcome, and ends with implications. For instance, rather than simply stating that a model improved fraud detection accuracy, the communicator could describe how this translated into reduced customer complaints, increased trust, and saved revenue. This storytelling approach makes the data feel tangible and relevant.

Timing and format also influence how insights are received. Presenting AI outcomes during high-level strategy meetings may call for concise executive briefs, while operational teams may require detailed walkthroughs during working sessions. Additionally, offering follow-up resources or one-on-one sessions for deeper clarification ensures stakeholders feel supported, not overwhelmed. The key is to foster an ongoing dialogue where data becomes a trusted tool in the decision-making process.

Finally, AI practitioners must be transparent about limitations and uncertainties. Overpromising can lead to distrust or misaligned expectations, especially if outcomes vary from projections. Communicating assumptions, confidence levels, data constraints, and potential risks builds credibility and enables stakeholders to make informed, nuanced decisions. When stakeholders are aware of what the AI can and cannot do, they are better equipped to integrate it into operational or strategic planning.

Communicating insights to non-technical stakeholders is not merely about simplifying language it is about building trust, encouraging informed engagement, and ensuring that AI serves real-world needs. In doing so, AI professionals not only deliver technical solutions but also foster shared understanding, alignment, and sustained impact across organizations.

Chapter 9

From Prototype to Production Execution Excellence

Building a successful AI solution goes far beyond constructing an accurate model in a sandbox environment. True value is only realized when a prototype matures into a production-ready system that integrates seamlessly into an organization's operations. This transition—from innovation to implementation—requires discipline, clarity, and a rigorous approach to execution. Chapter 9 explores the key principles and practices that govern the movement of AI projects from proof-of-concept to enterprise-scale deployment, with an emphasis on long-term usability, resilience, and return on investment.

The first step in achieving execution excellence is establishing a robust delivery pipeline. While early stages may focus on experimentation, a production-ready system demands structured workflows for data ingestion, model retraining, version control, and performance monitoring. Tools like CI/CD pipelines, model registries, and containerization ensure that the deployment process is automated, traceable, and repeatable. Moreover, integrating DevOps and MLOps practices enables technical teams to streamline releases, reduce error rates, and shorten iteration cycles. AI solutions must be able to evolve with changing data patterns, regulatory shifts, or business demands meaning production systems must be as dynamic as the environments they serve.

Second, organizations must address system integration at both the technical and operational level. AI systems rarely operate in isolation; they must connect with existing enterprise platforms, APIs, and dashboards. Integration success depends on modular design, standardized data schemas, and interoperable infrastructure. Just as important, the system must align with how teams make decisions—whether through alerts, scheduled reports, or automated workflows. A solution that delivers accurate results but fails to integrate into users' daily routines will remain underutilized. Therefore, production success hinges not just on code quality but on contextual relevance and user accessibility.

Another core pillar of execution excellence is governance. Once AI solutions move into production, questions of accountability, performance guarantees, and data stewardship become central. Who is responsible for monitoring model drift? How are data privacy risks mitigated? What thresholds trigger a retraining event? A successful deployment plan includes clear governance structures, incident response protocols, and compliance mechanisms. Organizations that treat AI systems as operational assets—not just experiments—tend to achieve better adoption, longevity, and strategic alignment.

Scalability and resilience are also critical. A model that works well for a limited use case must be re-engineered to handle higher data volumes, wider geographic coverage, or additional use scenarios. Infrastructure must support load balancing, failover, and real-time performance under pressure. This involves not just technical upgrades, but stress testing, scenario planning, and regular audits to ensure the system remains responsive and accurate under diverse conditions. Execution excellence means planning for durability ensuring AI can scale without compromising integrity.

Change management rounds out the execution journey. Rolling out a new AI system often requires organizational shifts in roles, processes, and workflows. Training, onboarding, and change communication are essential to ensure that end-users understand the system's purpose and are equipped to work alongside it.

Resistance to change is natural, but well-planned engagement strategies such as pilot phases, feedback loops, and champion user programs can accelerate adoption and reduce friction. AI is not a plug-and-play solution; it must be nurtured within the culture of its host environment.

From prototype to production, excellence in execution is what turns AI potential into tangible impact. It is where technical creativity meets operational discipline. As AI systems become more integral to core business operations across supply chain, healthcare, and finance, organizations that master this execution continuum will lead the next wave of intelligent transformation delivering not just innovation, but reliable, scalable, and sustainable performance.

Model Validation and Regulatory Compliance

Ensuring that AI models meet stringent validation requirements and align with regulatory expectations is a fundamental aspect of any successful production deployment. As industries like healthcare, finance, and supply chain increasingly rely on automated decision-making, the responsibility to validate model behavior, mitigate risk, and maintain transparency has never been greater. Without a clear framework for validation and compliance, even the most sophisticated AI system risks being underutilized or rejected entirely.

Model validation begins with defining performance criteria aligned with the intended business outcomes. This goes beyond accuracy and precision, encompassing fairness, bias mitigation, interpretability, and robustness under diverse real-world conditions. Internal validation teams must replicate real-use scenarios to test how the model behaves with edge cases, noisy data, or shifting patterns. Crucially, validation is not a one-time task; it requires continuous assessment to ensure models remain relevant and accurate as data evolves over time.

On the regulatory front, industries are governed by a patchwork of laws and standards that must be carefully navigated. In healthcare, regulations such as HIPAA demand strict safeguards for patient data privacy. In finance, institutions must comply with anti-money laundering protocols, fraud risk frameworks, and explainability requirements for automated decisions. Meanwhile, emerging AI regulations in regions like the European Union emphasize human oversight, algorithmic transparency, and the right to contest decisions. A model that lacks auditability or traceability can face serious compliance challenges, undermining trust and operational viability.

To address these risks, organizations must build compliance into their development and deployment lifecycle. This includes maintaining comprehensive documentation of training data, algorithmic choices, and version histories. It also means incorporating fairness audits, explainability tools, and feedback channels into the production pipeline. Regulatory alignment should not be an afterthought it must be embedded from the earliest design phase.

Achieving excellence in model validation and compliance ultimately protects both the organization and its end-users. It fosters accountability, enhances credibility, and paves the way for long-term operational success. In high-impact industries, where decisions affect lives, finances, and supply continuity, validated and compliant AI is not optional it is essential.

Managing Deployment and Monitoring Pipelines

Successfully deploying an AI model into production requires more than just high-performance metrics in a lab setting. It demands a robust, scalable, and maintainable deployment pipeline that can withstand real-world pressures and adapt to changing environments. In high-impact sectors like healthcare, finance, and supply chain management, the deployment phase must be tightly controlled to ensure operational continuity, data security, and regulatory adherence.

A key component of deployment management is automation. Using continuous integration and continuous deployment (CI/CD) frameworks allows teams to push model updates rapidly while maintaining consistency and traceability. This includes packaging models into containers, configuring APIs, and automating testing procedures to prevent regressions.

Deployment also involves integrating the model into existing infrastructure, whether that means embedding it into an enterprise resource planning system or interfacing with external data streams in real-time.

Equally critical is the establishment of monitoring pipelines. Once live, an AI model must be tracked for performance drift, data anomalies, latency, and error rates. Monitoring tools enable teams to detect when a model begins to underperform or when input data characteristics shift from training distributions a phenomenon known as concept drift. These monitoring systems must be equipped with alerting mechanisms that notify teams to retrain or adjust the model before business impact occurs.

Beyond technical indicators, monitoring should also account for user behavior and outcome validation. Are end-users interpreting predictions correctly? Are decisions leading to desired outcomes? Collecting this feedback helps organizations refine their models in context, closing the loop between prediction and performance.

To maintain long-term success, organizations should implement model governance practices that track version histories, manage rollback procedures, and ensure that every model iteration is thoroughly documented. This level of oversight not only improves operational transparency but also supports auditability and compliance efforts.

Ultimately, managing deployment and monitoring pipelines is about ensuring that AI systems remain reliable, responsive, and relevant. By investing in scalable deployment architecture and real-time monitoring, businesses can maximize the value of their models while minimizing risk a cornerstone of execution excellence in any data-driven enterprise.

Scaling Models Across Organizational Units

Scaling AI models across organizational units involves far more than replicating a successful prototype. It demands thoughtful coordination, adaptability to diverse operational contexts, and alignment with enterprise-wide goals. In high-impact sectors like healthcare, finance, and supply chain management, this process must be designed to preserve model integrity while enabling customization and responsiveness to local or departmental nuances.

One of the first challenges in scaling models is ensuring interoperability. Different units may use distinct data infrastructures, legacy systems, or third-party tools. To address this, organizations must invest in flexible integration frameworks that allow AI solutions to plug into various environments with minimal disruption. Using standardized APIs, modular architecture, and cloud-based platforms can significantly streamline this process.

Additionally, the success of a scaled deployment often hinges on collaboration between technical and non-technical stakeholders. Each unit may have unique performance metrics, user expectations, or regulatory constraints. Engaging local teams early, gathering contextual insights, and incorporating domain-specific feedback into model design helps ensure that the AI solution is not only accurate but also operationally relevant. This collaborative approach also drives greater user adoption, as teams are more likely to trust and use models they helped shape.

A robust data governance strategy is also essential for scaling. When AI models rely on inputs from multiple units, maintaining data consistency, quality, and compliance becomes critical. Clear policies around data ownership, access controls, and privacy safeguards must be established to support ethical and sustainable use of AI at scale.

Moreover, performance monitoring must be tailored to individual units. A model that performs well in one department may encounter challenges in another due to differences in workflows or data patterns. Customizing monitoring dashboards, establishing unit-specific benchmarks, and creating feedback loops ensure that models continue to deliver value across the organization.

Finally, scaling AI across an enterprise should be approached as a continuous process, not a one-time rollout. As business priorities evolve and external conditions shift, models must be recalibrated and retrained to stay aligned with organizational needs. This ongoing refinement transforms AI from a siloed innovation to a strategic enabler, creating a cohesive intelligence layer that connects and empowers every part of the organization.

Chapter 10

The Future of AI-Driven Transformation

Artificial intelligence has reached a pivotal point in its evolution. From experimental prototypes to enterprise-wide deployments, AI has proven its value across high-impact sectors such as supply chain, healthcare, and finance. However, the future of AI-driven transformation will not be defined solely by technological capability, but by how intelligently, responsibly, and inclusively it is applied. As the pace of innovation accelerates, leaders must look beyond isolated use cases and instead embrace AI as a foundational layer in long-term strategy, infrastructure planning, and societal progress.

One of the defining features of AI's future will be its convergence with other frontier technologies. The integration of AI with quantum computing, edge intelligence, and next-generation connectivity will enable decision-making at scales and speeds previously unattainable. In supply chain environments, for instance, this convergence could lead to self-optimizing logistics ecosystems capable of responding to geopolitical shifts, environmental factors, and market fluctuations in real time. AI will not only predict disruptions but orchestrate entire chains of action autonomously reshaping procurement, fulfilment, and inventory systems in profound ways.

In healthcare, the future of AI lies in precision, personalization, and prevention. Algorithms will move from supporting care delivery to actively managing health outcomes. Predictive diagnostics, real-time genomics, and patient-specific treatment planning will become standard practice. Hospitals and clinics will increasingly rely on intelligent systems to allocate resources, coordinate interventions, and minimize risk, while patients will engage with AI-powered tools for monitoring, self-care, and informed decision-making. As these shifts unfold, ethical frameworks and explainable AI models will be essential to maintain trust, safeguard data rights, and uphold the integrity of medical practice.

The finance sector is also entering a new era where AI will serve as a strategic differentiator rather than a tactical tool. Risk analytics will be continuously refined through deep learning and real-time behavioral modelling. AI will redefine fraud detection, not just flag anomalies but understanding intent and context. Moreover, financial institutions will evolve into intelligent organizations—deploying AI not only for operational efficiency but also to enhance customer experience, regulatory compliance, and long-term portfolio strategy. As algorithmic governance becomes standard, the ability to audit, validate, and transparently communicate AI's decisions will become an institutional priority.

Another critical dimension shaping the future of AI is its role in fostering inclusive and sustainable growth. Governments, civil society, and the private sector must collaborate to ensure that AI technologies do not widen inequality or perpetuate bias. Workforce transformation must accompany technological transformation. As AI automates repetitive tasks, new skills, jobs, and organizational models will emerge. The future will belong to institutions that prioritize reskilling, ethical innovation, and human-centered design. This is especially vital for emerging markets, where AI can unlock significant economic and developmental gains but only if deployed with awareness, equity, and accountability.

Finally, the future of AI-driven transformation depends on execution discipline and strategic foresight. Organizations must design AI systems not just to work but to evolve. Modular, scalable, and interoperable AI architectures will be necessary to adapt to changing requirements, regulatory shifts, and growing datasets. Success will hinge on cross-functional governance, responsible experimentation, and an unwavering commitment to long-term value. Those who embed AI as a strategic capability beyond tools or trends will redefine the frontier of what's possible in business, healthcare, and society.

In conclusion, the journey of AI has only just begun. The next phase is not about adoption it is about transformation. A future powered by AI will demand more than innovation; it will require vision, trust, and shared purpose. As we stand at this inflection point, the opportunity is clear: to design a future where intelligence, whether human or artificial, is directed toward solving real problems, empowering people, and creating a world that is not just smarter, but better.

Trends Shaping AI in Emerging Markets

Emerging markets are experiencing a rapid transformation driven by the proliferation of AI technologies. However, the trends shaping AI adoption and impact in these regions differ significantly from those observed in developed economies. The trajectory of AI in emerging markets is being shaped by a unique blend of opportunity, necessity, and ingenuity. From improving healthcare access to strengthening supply chains and digitizing financial ecosystems, AI is enabling scalable solutions tailored to local realities. These markets are not merely catching up they are innovating in context.

One of the most prominent trends is the rise of frugal AI—the development of cost-effective, resource-efficient models tailored for environments with limited infrastructure. Developers and data scientists in emerging regions are designing algorithms that run on low-power devices, require minimal data, and operate effectively in low-connectivity zones. This approach reflects a growing movement toward context-aware AI, where technological sophistication is balanced with practical deployment strategies. Frugal AI is particularly transformative in rural healthcare delivery, micro-logistics, and digital identity systems.

Another key trend is AI localization, where tools and interfaces are adapted for local languages, cultural nuances, and behavioral patterns. Natural language processing models are being trained to understand underrepresented dialects and regional idioms, enabling broader access to automated services such as chatbots, virtual assistants, and voice-based diagnostics. In multilingual and diverse countries, this trend is critical for expanding the reach of AI to underserved populations, reducing digital exclusion, and enhancing user engagement with intelligent systems.

Public-private collaboration is also emerging as a powerful trend in shaping the AI ecosystem in emerging markets. Governments, academic institutions, startups, and global tech companies are forming strategic partnerships to build data infrastructure, create innovation hubs, and offer capacity-building programs. These collaborations are essential for overcoming challenges related to data scarcity, policy gaps, and skill shortages. Countries like Nigeria, Kenya, and India are investing in AI strategies that align with national development goals, such as improving food security, urban planning, and disaster resilience.

Additionally, ethical innovation and responsible AI are becoming central themes in these markets. As AI solutions scale across sectors, questions around bias, data privacy, and algorithmic fairness are gaining prominence. Innovators in emerging markets are not only borrowing best practices from global frameworks but also developing region-specific governance models to ensure that AI is deployed in a socially responsible manner. This includes community-led data stewardship initiatives, local advisory boards, and AI literacy campaigns aimed at fostering public trust.

Lastly, entrepreneurial adaptation is defining the character of AI development in emerging economies. Startups and social enterprises are using AI to solve hyperlocal problems—from optimizing informal transport systems to automating agricultural diagnostics for smallholder farmers. These ventures often operate with lean resources but demonstrate high levels of creativity and agility. Their success underscores the idea that innovation is not bound by wealth or infrastructure—it thrives where people combine vision with urgency.

In summary, the trends shaping AI in emerging markets reveal a future where intelligence is inclusive, decentralized, and deeply responsive to real-world needs. These regions are not passive recipients of AI technologies—they are actively shaping its evolution in ways that may serve as a blueprint for global application.

Human-AI Synergy in Decision-Making

As artificial intelligence continues to mature, the narrative is shifting from automation versus human labour to collaboration between intelligent systems and human judgment. In high-impact industries such as healthcare, supply chain, and finance, the future lies not in replacing human decision-makers but in enhancing their capabilities through AI-powered insights. This synergy between human intuition and machine precision is redefining how decisions are made, improving speed, accuracy, and contextual awareness while retaining essential human values like empathy, ethics, and situational understanding.

One of the most promising dimensions of human-AI synergy is in augmented intelligence, where AI does not act autonomously but functions as a co-pilot. In healthcare, for example, AI systems analyze medical images and patient histories to suggest diagnoses, while physicians provide the final interpretation based on nuanced patient interactions. This collaborative model improves diagnostic accuracy and reduces cognitive load without undermining the role of the clinician. It ensures that complex decisions benefit from the computational power of AI without losing the depth of human experience.

In the financial sector, AI-driven advisory tools support decision-making in areas like investment planning, fraud detection, and credit risk assessment. These systems can process thousands of variables and detect subtle patterns, flagging anomalies that human analysts might miss. However, human oversight remains critical to interpret these patterns within broader economic, ethical, and regulatory contexts. The most effective systems combine AI-generated probabilities and recommendations with domain expertise to support responsible and balanced choices.

The supply chain industry offers another vivid example of this synergy. Logistics managers use AI to forecast demand, predict supply disruptions, and recommend optimal routing strategies. While the models suggest best-case scenarios based on data, it is human leaders who contextualize these insights against real-time developments such as political changes, cultural factors, or force majeure events. This shared decision-making process creates a dynamic environment where neither machine nor human operate in isolation but rather in complement.

Trust and transparency are vital in sustaining this synergy. For human stakeholders to rely on AI tools in critical decision-making, they must understand how models reach their conclusions. Explainable AI (XAI) frameworks are being integrated into systems to provide justifications in human-readable language. This allows users to question, refine, and even override decisions, ensuring accountability and fostering a culture of continuous learning between humans and machines.

Ultimately, human-AI synergy reflects a deeper philosophical shift: one that views intelligence not as a zero-sum contest but as a collaborative capacity distributed across minds and machines. The convergence of AI systems with human decision-making frameworks holds the potential to elevate organizational outcomes, reduce bias, and unlock new levels of insight. As AI becomes more embedded in enterprise strategy, this synergy will be central to building resilient, adaptive, and ethically sound systems for the future.

Roadmap for Sustainable AI Impact

Creating long-term, positive outcomes from artificial intelligence requires more than technical proficiency it demands a clear, strategic roadmap rooted in sustainability, equity, and ethical design. In high-impact sectors such as healthcare, finance, and supply chain, the focus is shifting from experimental deployments to building AI ecosystems that consistently deliver value while minimizing harm. A roadmap for sustainable AI impact addresses not only how models are built and deployed, but also how they evolve, integrate, and contribute to systemic progress over time.

The first step in this roadmap involves developing AI systems with purpose-driven intent. This means aligning every project with defined social, operational, or strategic objectives that extend beyond immediate performance metrics. In healthcare, for instance, AI should not only streamline diagnostic procedures but also close disparities in access to quality care. In finance, models must reduce fraud without reinforcing historical biases that penalize certain demographics. Sustainable impact begins by asking not just what AI can do, but what it should do—and for whom.

Governance and lifecycle accountability are essential pillars of sustainable AI development. Organizations must create frameworks for monitoring AI systems post-deployment, ensuring they remain relevant, fair, and aligned with evolving regulatory and ethical standards. This includes establishing multidisciplinary oversight committees, regularly auditing data sources for bias, and investing in retraining models as business conditions change. Rather than treating AI implementation as a one-off initiative, the roadmap advocates for continuous feedback loops between outcomes, users, and technical teams.

Next is the critical need to embed environmental sustainability into AI infrastructure. Training deep learning models consumes significant energy, raising concerns about AI's carbon footprint. Companies committed to responsible innovation are now optimizing model efficiency, using renewable-powered data centers, and choosing leaner architectures that balance performance with sustainability. For example, instead of training massive models from scratch, organizations are increasingly using transfer learning and federated learning approaches that reduce energy and data dependency.

Scalability without exclusion is another key principle. To ensure that AI benefits are widespread, solutions must be designed to operate in low-resource environments as effectively as in advanced ones. This involves creating modular, adaptable systems that work with limited bandwidth, smaller datasets, and minimal hardware. In Africa, Asia, and Latin America, such approaches are already making AI accessible in rural clinics, small financial cooperatives, and grassroots supply chains demonstrating that impactful AI need not be exclusive or capital-intensive.

Finally, sustainable AI impact rests on collaborative ecosystems. No single company or sector can unlock the full potential of artificial intelligence. Governments, academia, startups, and civil society must work together to set shared standards, pool resources, and co-create platforms that foster responsible use.

Public-private partnerships can drive the development of open data platforms, accessible tools, and inclusive talent pipelines. These collaborations are vital for ensuring that AI advances do not concentrate power but instead contribute to distributed, resilient progress.

A sustainable AI future is one where innovation is not only continuous but conscientious where data systems are as inclusive as they are intelligent, and where business value aligns with societal good. The roadmap toward this future is not linear, but it is navigable with vision, responsibility, and coordinated action guiding every step.

www.ingramcontent.com/pod-product-compliance
Lightning Source LLC
Chambersburg PA
CBHW021214250926
51852CB00006B/7
9783672739782